In the Cities of Sleep

Russian River

Napa River

tsêmanoma

Mark West Creek

annakótanoma

tóhrakau

cutáwani

wílak

hukabeíyant

Sonoma Creek

maskawáni

akapólowani

wilikos

káimus

bútakatcatchani

Laguna de Santa Rosa

lumentakala

bóhosole

kotâti

Sonoma Mountain

ulíyami

oona-pa'is

payinetca

wugilili

tuli'

húici

susúli

témble

túme

tutcaiyélin

petalúma

súskol

meléya

étem

Petaluma River

amayélle

tolay

olompólli

tcokéttce

Sonoma
Mountain
Native Lands
of the
Miwok & Pomo

0   2   4 Miles

Ален Young 2022. Data Sources: Esri, SF El, Arthur Dawson.
Wikipedia Map of the territory of the Pomo linguistic stock

In the Cities of Sleep

Elizabeth C. Herron

Fernwood
PRESS

In the Cities of Sleep
©2023 by Elizabeth C. Herron

Fernwood Press
Newberg, Oregon
www.fernwoodpress.com

Printed in the United States of America

Cover and interior design: Mareesa Fawver Moss
Cover photo: Zoltan Tasi
Cartography: Alex Young alexyoung@gmail.com

ISBN 978-1-59498-097-8

To my beloved *onna-pa'is*, Sonoma Mountain
and the Atascadero, whose soil and water smell of home.

Ladybug, ladybug, fly away home,
your house is on fire, your children will burn.

Traditional nursery rhyme

I want you to act as if the house was on fire.
Because it is.

Greta Thunberg

CONTENTS

We were happily motes on spears of sun
in the morning of it all.
We were earth and tree and sky and sea
and drifted all unknowing
in the Goldilocks Range of Eden.

Before

Solastalgia

Once we were Earth
was beautiful
was water
flowers
under sea
in forest even
here
blossom and bee all shaped in lovely
and dancing in flit and suck and honey
and languid-limbed we brought forth
and died back
in our season and lived again
in the long line of mother to Mother
Earth,
to seed to flame of spring—
in balance did we
in balance
and beauty.
Once we were.
Was beautiful.

Swan Bone

The bones of birds
being hollow
for obvious reasons,
it might be obvious also
why the first flutes
found thousands of years after
the pentatonic melodies they played
in the lives
of *Homo Sapien Neanderthalensis*
and *Homo Sapien Sapiens,*
perhaps while dancing,
perhaps while there was chanting
around them, perhaps
while the dancers
moved in circles,
perhaps while someone else
shook a rattle, and someone
struck a drum, and a boy
in the circle of dancers
looked up to a cloud of swans
traversing the autumn—
their hollow wing-bones
lifting and falling
above a swirl of yellow leaves
that smoked the sky
with gold.

Report

February. Moon of the Long Snow.
Wind from the northwest.

In the bowl of the Big Dipper,
the Lesser Lion's diamond appears,
faded slightly ragged-maned
under a full moon ascending
over *oona-pa'is*
where Coyote made the world
with a feather.

The wind blows east
across the San Andreas fault.

Clouds gather behind the plum boughs.

In the crevices
of the body,
petals open
and fall.

Mountains.
Full moon.
Haiku of the hips.

Mars rising at 4 a.m.
follows Venus across the heavens,
high over the mountain
where a black-tail doe
steps quietly into the dark trees.

*

Eastern Pacific ocean current,
swinging south along the continental shelf.
Gyre of salmon,
swimming 'round the clock.
The shelf falls steeply into blue salt.

*

Prayers to the air may be uttered at dusk,
at moonrise, at midnight,
and again at dawn, regardless of showers.

Lesser Lion claws the sky.
The body sighs. Petals fall
in the crevices.

At dawn the roshi rakes
the gravel path outside the zendo, there—
her tracks, the doe
who crossed under stars
to bed down in the trees.

*

One plate meets another in a rift
a half-mile wide, the deep cleft
of the Pacific sliding for eons
under the North American. Up

in the Aleutian Islands, the subduction
eases its way with less friction
than you might imagine,
considering the weight
and occasional bursts
of volcanic activity in these

hot zones—the hips, tongue,
and southern areas
of the body calling Venus

to rise behind veils
of smoke. Ash
falls in the crevices,
building over time
into layers of rock.
Everything a process—

Laetoli footprints,
continental drift—
a heart
exploding from center

expresses heat
in magma rising easy
and red as Mars
through all weather.

6-foot swells, westerly winds,
the falling, the sinking, the unrelenting
eternal
heat.

    *

(Jupiter's moons)

Volcanic calderas in a region near
the south pole of Io. Also cliffs
and lava flows partly obscured
by gauzy mists. She spins

in the orbit of an expansive planet—
Jupiter, the open heart, the overflowing
coffer, the kingdom's king. Io

circles in a passion expressed
by her Vulcan possibilities.
She squanders heat. She twists
under her mists of steam.
The king smiles

confused. Isn't that his daughter?
Mystified by her
ecstatic expression.
Io, unaware of his uncertainty,
faithful to his insistent gravity,

leans and spins and casts her billows—
too small in spite of her lolling calderas,
in spite of her regional heat,
in spite of her twisting and rolling.

Jupiter sets at 8:46 as if he were aging.
Io and Europa, urgent under ice,
under hot lava,
spitting and freezing
while the waves push and suck,
rise and fall, rolling the sea's drum.

    *

Deep in the rift zone, a slow heat
builds that remains undetectable.
The lovers tremble as the crust shifts.

A weak high-pressure ridge builds
over the Redwood region
ahead of an approaching trough.

Venus rises. 4-foot waves and 6-foot swells
lift from the ocean and tidal pools
of the body, heart
of the salt born blood in 12-knot winds.

Sunny skies

belie the approaching storm, the rising
wind, the waves. Temperatures dropping
from 50 to 40 to 30 degrees.

West of the Big Dipper's bowl, the Lynx,
a long faint constellation, crouches
above Leo.

Behind the incoming spatter of rain,
the Magellanic Clouds continue to swirl.

Europa, in all her distance,
remains under ice.

The Lion's paws grip cumulonimbus.
Petals fall. The shelf drops sharply
into blue salt. Her crevices
salty sweet. Blue heart, blue lake
of longing.

*

In rest—like the space
between stars or heartbeats—

uncertainty hinges. There,
Coyote waves his feather wand.

Venus rises at 6 a.m. Petals
open. The moon,
a raucous blare, moves west.

Blue salt, blue dusk, blue lake
of longing.

Temperatures over the region drop
to 30 degrees in the dawn low.

Venus, her crevices
effaced by distance,
closes her lamp against the wind,

though she does not waver
through the long day.

A thin confetti of petals
below the apple tree.

*

(Hubble's revelations)

Six billion years ago seen now
through the curve of time—
pillars of dark gas announce
another star birth. The far light arrives
or arriving still, like desire,

swelling to 8 feet, sweeping toward shore,
swirled in the body's scents, the humors
of passion. Early galactic formation,
nascent embryonic events,
a million light years hence becoming

visible—
the morphology of genesis revealed,
the evolution of divine desire,
hurling fragments of shifting matter,
black holes, and murk.

Europa seething, Io in her scarves,
clings to Jupiter. Mars follows Venus
over the horizon
just after dark. The pull of gravity,

greater with proximity.
The ardor of distant bodies,
the unforgettable longing of light

despite the ice, despite rain.

*

March. Moon of softening soil,
the Worm Moon of spring.

Continuing low-pressure trough
pulls cold over the Eastern Pacific,
unseasonable snow to the northwest, drifts
over the Mayacamas, a chill
onshore, wind and rain tonight,
heavy at times.

Road closures throughout the Redwood Empire.
Deer shelter under new sprigs of willow.
Lows in the 40s. Pockets of cold dropping
the heart to sub-zero for the season.

The bright Capella de Auriga, the Charioteer
high in the northwest, his thighs
gripping the sky, hands on the empty reins,

briefly shares the heavens with Jupiter
and Mars. Venus rises early, settles back
to a clear sky as the heart surges
seaward in moon-pulled darkness.

The Milky Way ribbons behind mostly
cloudy skies. Hearts humming
all night,

the lovers listen for rain,
blessed by the long bones of darkness,
a stipple of stars behind closed lids.

In the early morning hours,
rain sweeps in, locally heavy
as the storm circles south.

*

November. Full moon again.
Blue heart, blue salt, blue lake
of longing.

Tangle of legs, arms, salty sweet—
iambic heart.

Capella de Auriga circles the pole
round and round, night after night,
hopelessly caught in the unending arc
of the search for his lost horses.

The wind sweeps east. The roshi rakes
outside the zendo.

Restless, magnetic north shifts
under Arctic water,
over Earth's fiery heart, magma
rolling under blankets of blue and green.

The swell of desire,
the swift and fleeting satisfaction.

A low pressure trough lingers,
keeping rain over the Empire.

Mars sets at 9:25. Clouds
obscure the dazzling fireworks
in the constellation Aquilla
where excitement rivals
the streets and ring of Pamplona.

Stars and the sparks of castanets.

Hubble's breathtaking views,
deeper than ever into the heavens.

Rings of glowing hot gas, unimaginable
here in the cool tremors of leaf buds
and grasses bravely pushing

through autumn's silver-gray.
Along the Atascadero, ghost mist
rises at dusk.

26

Between

February Freeze

One February morning, we found
three dead birds in the orchard,

not a mark on them, frozen in flight,
migrating at night, wings

beating the dark
till they dropped like fallen stars,

their bones turned to ice.
I thought of those birds again

when the Eritrean who spent
seven years seeking legal entry

to Switzerland before he stowed away
in the wheel-well of a Boeing 747

was found frozen, fallen
to an English village street.

Dial Face

for Ken Saro-Wiwa

Before dawn—she stirs the embers,
singing softly for her daughter.

Shush-whiz of morning commute,
wheels turning, numbers changing.

The parts of a gasoline pump
include the dial face

where numbers roll,
tracking gallons, dollars—

not the hands holding plastic bottles
and tin cups under the leaking pipeline,

not the lives that don't count.

From the highway, traffic picks up—
wheels whirring, numbers changing.

Her face bright in firelight,
she stirs the embers in the morning,

singing softly for the daughter
who vanished into bits one might

have recognized—a small hand reaching,
brown eyes

still as the dials
when the pump clicks off.

Eremocene

for E. O. Wilson

The ice melt leaves the walrus
homeless, and thousands climb out
of the sea onto Arctic beaches.
If each of us carried our own
dark stones, held them close,
called them by name, and blamed
no one, if the heart
could stay open,
if we sang prayers
and praises for the sea ice
and the walrus,
for the caribou
calving, the sheltering trees
and the red squirrels in the morning,
the Earth's great ice
might gather again and the world
spin its seasons, wealthy
with its own ever-becoming.

Ghost Dance

Quiet spaces in the mind
wide as the Great Plains

into the bell jar of the cell phone,
into the places of black stone.

In Nebraska and Kansas,
the harvester pitches over acres

pocked for thousands of years
by burrows and warrens that caught the rain
for the Ogallala aquifer.

The harvester shambles on,
lumbering over the bones of the buffalo,
grinding over the quiet spaces in the mind

of the First Nations—the Lakota,
the Cheyenne, and the Comanche
whose Ghost Dancers chanted
to restore their lost world:

Father, give us back our arrows.

Stones,
black stones,
machines, and silicone chips.

How will we live
without the quiet
spaces in the mind?

In the far cities
under indifferent towers
that hunt our sleep and glean our dreams,

harvesting the algorithms
of the twenty-first century,
the cash register rings

in the irregular rhythm
of the ghost dance
of zeros.

Migrants

Open water
The slap of the Mediterranean
A photograph
One among many

Man Found on Fire

We thought it was a Christmas tree until it moved.
Officer Faenetta Hutchings, SFPD

Arms flung out
like heavy branches,
he blazed.
His clothes billowed
with the rush
of trapped air
between the layers
of jackets and shirts,
oversized trousers
on their last legs,
running shoes
melting onto the soles
of his feet.
His head was the star,
they thought,
sparks flying
from his hair.
Silent
as he burned,
he finally moved
to alert them
he was human.
Henry Williams,
burning at the bus stop
at 4:45 a.m.,
was unable to tell officers
how he caught fire.

The Virus on Good Friday

Of the ten, seven were black.
I ate them first. They were sweet
to the marrow.

Two of the ten were brown
and tasted of wax
with a pinch of gunpowder.
They sang and prayed as I chewed
them up.

One of the ten was a white man.
I knew he'd be dry
as overdone turkey.

I had expected lamb,
but the most tender meat I got
was his son, forgiveness
in his nature (not mine)—
he tasted of tears and vinegar.

A red buzz occupied the city.
That was the music
and no dancing at all!

Unless you count
the Russian ballerinas
who took pots and pans for partners.
It was spring,

and a new hunger
was spinning in my belly.

Dancing in the Time of Covid

Outside, the air
smells of the neighborhood—
meat on a grill,
the scent of Julia's laundry soap
beside Marge's wisteria,
wood fires,
the smoke
above John and Michelle's house—
one village,
over the fences and down the alley,
under a low gray sky,
wet streets,
the plain mud
of our common lives.
One village,
everybody home,
the virus out there,
who knows where,
and just now,
suppertime
quiet.
We don't go out,
live on cabbage and pickled beets,
broccoli and tree collards,
potatoes and onions pulled up
from the winter garden,
tea and honey.
Nobody nothing life of mine
dancing in the hallway.

Grandmothers

They've been through other pandemics.
Somebody's great uncle died,
blood-black with the Spanish flu.

They remember the stories.
In time, they say—but

some things take your hope
the way the wind takes a candle, and you
don't have another match.

The virus eels from one mutation
to another, quick and dangerous.
The season's shadows give way
to light, and still the virus shape-shifts.

The post office closed last month. Today,
someone tossed a rock through the window.

While Bombs Fell

For weeks while bombs fell in Aleppo
and rockets exploded the dark
and birds flew blind from the trees,
you dreamed of books—
the entire library of human history
afloat on the ocean.

The birds
thrown upward in the flare, balanced
on the explosion's apex of air
till their wings flew away
from their bodies,

as the pages floated away
from their bindings
soaked in salt,
words without context: here
Hannibal's army riding elephants over the Alps,
there Hildegard von Bingen's musical notations.

One thousand Americans died of drug overdose
in those two weeks, while the bombs
dropped over Syria,
and the birds plummeted
soundlessly with only
an explosion of feathers.
Their wings sailed on the turbulence,
then fluttered down
to rubble and dust.

The hands
fell from the needles
like the wings off a bird.
The pages sailed away, balanced
on the current and salt of the tide
before they sank. *How cunning,*
you said when you woke—*the way*
things come apart, the way they change
from something to nothing.

Strike *to do the digging*

I rummage in the kitchen
all hours—3 a.m.
under the overhead light,
looking for sleep

in cheap brandy
to wash the wreckage
of trapped feelings
down my throat.

The bodies of crushed cars
and collapsed buildings
close the street.
I don't have the machines,

the local authority reported—
a dozer groans
as it shoves rubble
to clear the path

for an ambulance.
Even if
I were to consider, he said—
the dozer pushes ahead of its blade

broken pottery, splintered
timbers and shattered stone,
dented pots and pans, a single
dust-dry sandal with twisted

straps. Neighbors picking through
have found the woolen cap
of a missing boy,
and the animal grief pours forth

in a foreign tongue.
I pour the brandy
in my 3 a.m. kitchen.
I don't scream or cry.

Nesting

. . . turning round and round and pressing back the walls
on every side . . . exercising an active pressure . . . .
Thus, the nest is made.

I.

The two species met in argument
over the site, a sapling black oak—
the hawk, each feather limned
by the blank blue sky, flapping
furiously while the jay made fast
for the inner branches. There,
the larger bird lost his advantage
and was forced to give up
the attack and relinquish the tree.

2.

Vocalizations may include moans
accompanied by dramatic gestures
normally considered unusual, even
bizarre—the mouth, the breast,
the posterior.

3.

Nesting activities among mammals often involve
conversation. The female may yip, cough,
or whine seductively, urging the male
to heights of participation previously
unimagined. Males have been known
to labor long through the summer evenings,
carrying articles to and fro for the female, who
selects and discards.

4.

This instinct, said to be strongest
during the reproductive periods
of an organism's life, seems sometimes
to prevail beyond apparent usefulness.
A woman, for instance, past

her reproductive years, might continue
to expand her nesting activity, spending
unusual amounts of time (which can be
calculated and quantified by hours and seasons)
to demonstrate an even stronger nesting
impulse than many fertile females.

Everything, he noted, *is a matter of inner pressure,
physically dominant intimacy. The nest is a swelling fruit,
pressing against its limits.*

5.

The female, assuming an appearance
of complete relaxation, settles
into the structure. Her visible receptivity
(the result of pervasive cellular softening
entirely instinctive and accompanied
by a deep sense of well-being
and absence of ambition) is then
most likely to accept impregnation.

*The house is a bird's very person . . . I shall even say,
its suffering. The result is only obtained by constantly
repeated pressure of the breast.*

6.

Carried to extremes, the efforts
of such women move past their gardens
and may result in a preoccupation
with the larger purview
of the world itself, as if the nest

were the entire Earth. Once adopted,
this view causes subjects
such concern over the fate of the nest
that activities assume an urgency,
potentially disrupting matters of state.

7.

The nest, intended as the protective structure
for incubation, birth, safety, security,
and the general welfare of young, faces
unexpected threats.

The mallards, having nested
for several generations along the marsh,
were unable to anticipate
agricultural practices that included mowing
the riparian fringe. Thus, the pair wander
amid the slain grass, dazed
by the absence of their nest, the disappearance
of their eggs.

8.

What could be more blunt
than a bullet?

The mother in her kitchen,
unable to avert its arc

through an open window
(the only slant to this truth),

her eleven-year-old daughter
dead
        on impact.

9.

Salted with tears, the gardens
of the elder women
give such a harvest as arises
only from anguish, the ripening of which
yields a bitterness more strengthening
than the sweetest fruit or the hardiest root,
although it grows from their weeping
for the empty places
(the marshes, the kitchens)
where lost generations linger.

10.

The mother in her kitchen,
the clatter of pots and pans, the spilled
water darkening the clay floor, the child
lying amid shattered plates—
the sparrow-body's narrow chest shudders
closed, wings folding,
the heart   stops
under its slight moon of ribs.

II.

Department of Public Health and Welfare reports
struggles for resources and political power
as well as rogue viruses
may interrupt the social order
to a profound degree with displaced populations,
complicated grief, loss
of cultural restraints
accompanied by increased rape
and infant abandonment
as well as a significant rise in maternal mortality
and various disorders of traumatic stress.

e.g. - intermittent sniper fire stabs the street
    - the mallards circle slowly through the cut grass
    - weeping, the women search the rubble
    - unable to find his family, the child wanders the
      countryside
    - young men roam in bands, breaking windows
      and attacking strangers
e.g. - elder women rise from their gardens,
      tearing their hair

12.

As the ribs make a cradle for the heart,

as a cradle is a kind of nest,

as from tendings, beginnings may arise,

as when cupped around a candle
or especially when paired, the hands
may be said to make a nest,

as this morning, forming a prayer,
fingers extended and tipped up together,
I hold between my palms
the still-warm red-dyed egg.

A Woman Lies Still

for Oleksandra Matviichuk

I start with the weeds I know
will seed first
and tug them up
from thick spring ground

while six thousand miles,
on the other side of the Earth,
a woman drops and flattens herself
against mud and melting snow
at the side of the road.

I turn my ear to the ground,
as if I could hear the war
that keeps her pressed to the ditch.

The hood of her prettiest parka,
with the white faux fur trim,
settles to the mud, and she doesn't stir.
For hours, she lies on the cold,
her suitcase spilled open beside her,
listening
to the roar and whine of rockets
and bullets.

The hawk,
calling all morning, is suddenly
silent, and I go in. Peace
is a quiet presence
in my kitchen. Only the light
has changed.

Children of War

Daughter

She offers them—her arms,
her hands, fingers spread, the black

gates of her elbows locked open.
She begs you to take them.

Her head tilts back, throat
exposed. Even there, she is burned.

In the narrow room
beside the metal bed,

I bend to kiss the only place
the fire has left for me.

The soles of my daughter's feet
smell of rubber and seared lamb,

taste of smoke, dirt, and the grit
of broken concrete.

Brother

Outside the crumbling walls,
I harvest rusty screws,

bottle caps, even gravel
into an old soup can

I take to the others, hiding
under the wide tongue of tin

in the rubble where the school was.
I still hear her scream

above the howl of the bombs,
and I don't care whose fault this is.

I am becoming the flame itself,
pure and without mercy.

Son

The plastic Evian bottle
packed with rusty screws

skids, exploding
on the first bounce half-way back

in the bed of the truck,
and all he remembers

is flying and the blue, blue,
endless blue—why

hadn't he seen how blue it was,
how inside it he is,

like being inside
robin's egg blue,

his mother called it,
the broken shell she showed him.

The nest had fallen in the spring storm.
I saw the robin, she said,

sitting on the branch above.
It looked confused.

The shell was paper thin and smaller
than he would have thought,

but now, the egg is enormous.
Everything is inside it. The debris

falling around him is only
the brown specks he saw

on the outside of the broken shell—
delicate enough to make him cry

because now he is a boy again,
and this is the last thing he sees.

Because now he sees that he is
inside everything, and everything

is inside him, and he is looking down—
he has become the robin, no,

he is the small splotch of yolk
he dipped his finger in—

it was golden yellow as the sun,
so close the light is everywhere

blinding him. It was golden,
darker than the yellow on a

bumblebee, the color of calendula
in the garden by the rope

swing. He is swinging
higher than he ever has before,

into the blue
between the speckles now.

There is nothing
between him and the yellow,

yellow sun, and he is letting go
the rope, he is flying.

Cell Songs

I.

Encoded in the nucleus of every cell,

in the DNA is a song—
so long as the cells hold their shape,
your body making music,
dead or alive,

the song slowing as the cells dissolve.

Years from now   traces of melody
still exist   in a hair
clinging to the jacket you left
on the bus.   Think of it,

the entrainment/harmony
of your body singing

beside your lover   the elfin melody
of the baby at your breast
or the bright notes
of the monthly red seeping
of the woman you live with—

thus our intimacies reach through
the body's boundaries.   From a lost cell,
a prayer can rest its hand on your heart,
a song from worlds away can smooth

an errant illness back to proper pattern,
  lungs elastic for their honeycomb
of air   their shuffling back and forth
on the shore of breath.

2.

The boy smell.   Over and over, you said,
pick up your clothes   please
put your clothes in the laundry.

Wishing now for one unwashed shirt,
just one   to have back the boy
grown   who
stood in the doorway   a stranger,
   the boy smell gone.   The man now
gone   still,

the song of his cells humming
from the comb in a drawer
or his old baseball glove.

One unwashed shirt   his smell,
his song still there.

3.

(Even the small body
of a road-killed mouse
has a fading melody.)

4.

This is where he walked
before the explosion   the bomb
strapped to his body.   He walked
to the bridge   alone,
walked out of life   out of your life.
toward a deafening   giving all the songs
to the wind.   If you are very quiet,
you can hear them.

Your heart broken open, the music
from the empty glove. You hold
his comb   his song.   Lost,
his lost smell some-
where. His song somewhere.   If only
you had one unwashed shirt.

5.

Here is the place where the children
were crossing.   The bridge
is gone   now.   A chorus
lifts from rubble   their songs
high and clear and sweet
as spring water.

6.

A single bomb
strapped to the body,

the children coming home
from school.

7.

This is the hospital where they took them.
The ventilators are quiet now.

This is the road where the convoy
took a wrong turn.

He threw a rock.

The cluster bombs looked like toys.

They were in the house next door.

The rebels fired from the school.

It was an accident.

8.

So many sundered songs—

what we know of pain   how surprise
crafts confusion

how the ground hums with dissolving,

all our songs   stopped finally
in the earth's closed mouth.

If Only

Happy years of research
finally published—everything
we wanted to know
and more. All made possible
with funding from disinterested
sources, made sensible
with graphs and charts, apexes and nadirs,
percentages and arrows indicating
possible outcomes.

Just kept forgetting and remembering
and forgetting again the data buried
in the majestic lingo
of science. Who cared
if the ice was melting?
Who cared if you forgot your mask?

If only our female pelvises
had not narrowed
when we got on our own two feet
and walked out into the savannah
and got our thumbs
to go every which way,
we could still be swinging in the trees!

I wouldn't be whittling away
my days scratching out this translation.
The virus would have cooked
in the bodies of bats, and the guns
would have waited forever,
just chunks of innocent iron in the earth.

If only Coyote had stayed back
by the long shadows. If only
he hadn't gotten hold of that stick
of sunlight.

Smoke

The girls hold their cigarettes
outside the open windows of the car
pulled to the side of the road,
engine running as they smoke.

Fires burning miles to the east
smudge the sun orange. They smoke
out of their uneasy knowing
it's all connected—the fire,

the fracking boomtowns, the children
dying a world away because
a war is going on, because the river
is salted by a rising sea,

because those hospitals
have no antiviral, because the farm
is a desert now. They know
there are children behind a chain-link fence

who remember prayers
in another language. These children
are not so far away. Their faces
flash across the internet

and television news.
The girls hold their cigarettes out
the windows so their hair won't smell
like smoke. They smoke because

they're scared of what they see.
Blown from the eastern fires,
smoke sticks in a haze of ash
to the windshield. They've heard

it carries the dust of the dead
along with toxic particles
of plastic and melted metal—
carpeting, refrigerators, cars—

always cars now, the air
more dangerous than their cigarettes.
From space, the lines of fire
appear like the bright ragged hem

of an irregular coastline.
Thirteen billion years ago,
the lights came on in the universe
with the fiery birth of stars.

On Fire

A deer catches fire, no—
the fire catches her,
wicks up her body,
and she becomes the flame

for an instant, her bones white,
then black and crumbling,
becoming ash, then
pure heat—

the exquisite bristling fur
of the cinnamon bear glows
from his rounded back,
his paws raised,
each claw a candle,

the rabbit, bobcat, and mouse,
their whiskers bright
and fine as the lines of a web,

the spiders are just sparks
blown skyward—
no separate existence,
one with the God of Fire,

a hungry roar
leaping through trees,
racing the grasses,
utterly free and unforgiving.

Winter Pilgrims

The form of a pilgrimage is makeshift.
  Ronald Grimes

First were the boats—
rafts, dories, even an inner-tube
in the Mediterranean. A boy
washed up face-down in Greece.
Innumerable rescues and many
too late, bodies floating
like fallen feathers. The diaspora
of the twenty-first century begins to jumble—
Iraq, Syria, Sudan, Afghanistan, Nigeria—
they come in waves over land and water.
I wanted to write about them,

the refugees, though no one wants to call them that.
Refugees have rights. Migrants
are flightless birds, spoiled fruit, parts
of broken promises—pressed between countries,
between civil collapse and the loss
of arable land—I saw them

on the television in the Nissan Sales and Service lobby
with the sound off,
                    thousands
gathered in the winter woods
with their meager consolation of thin jackets
and small fires and thin blue tents,

the same blue tents we see along our freeways
where P2P-meth users huddle against the sear
of uselessness, discarded lives in blue tents
                                        everywhere,
                        here
                and there
in the winter woods,
without food, with snow the only water—
I saw them
                on the TV
                        with the sound off.

Tired of waiting,
my car still not ready,
I walked through November's dusk
to the closest coffee shop—a Starbucks—
as the tipped cup of the moon came up
above the neon strip of auto row.
There she is, I thought, *the silver lady*
pouring her light

on the busy street,
on the blue tents by the overpass,
and on him—the boy with the animal-ears cap
I'd seen on TV in his father's arms,
facing a wall of razor wire.
I wanted to write about them,
to report from one human to another

about those people in the forest.
An infant who died of exposure is buried there
and a Syrian man who drowned in the border river.
There were others too.
The silver lady spilled her cup
on their graves. Days later, her light

floods the woods, floods over the snow
stained by their pilgrimage
and over the abandoned debris, the residue
of their defeat, evidence of their presence
and their departure. Could you say,
in a manner of speaking,
from the heart,
that now those woods are a makeshift sacred ground?

I wanted to write about them,
our brothers and sisters seeking milk and honey
or just a job
and a plate of crappy food
and a safe place to sleep. Or just
to get out of the killing cold.

I wanted to write about the blue tents—
to say those people matter.
I wanted to mark the time and place—
mine walking to Starbucks
and theirs

on the border of Poland and Belarus
and in the no-man's-land beside the freeway—
all of us
under the same silver lady.
I wanted to say these people are strangers
only because we have yet to recognize
ourselves.

Here Now

No matter the sharp clean line
of a roof against blue,
between earth and sky
exploding,
this bruise-able earth
keeps singing no matter—
the deep pocks
in the eastern wheat fields,
no matter the empty bowl of Africa,
no matter the bones of Babi Yar
and Stalin's cold hand at the throat,
the stolen wheat
stolen again—
no matter the postman with his bag of letters
scattered across the snow.
A world away
from the blood-lands,
a child is walking home
with a pink backpack of books,
and standing under the apple tree,
the wayward reaching blossoms
of mock orange
in the quiet garden,
we are safe,
blessed
with this house, this spring,
the blood of First People
long-since soaked
into this soil. We are here now
with the rich scent of rain
and plenty of plenty.

The High Window

for Majid-Reza Rahnavard

The darkness of winter coats, leather belts, blue
gun barrels, and coffee. He did not refuse it.

In the beginning, they spoke gently.
It's not a problem, they said, blue guns

asleep in their black leather beds,
pouring the coffee, solicitous: *Sugar? More sugar?*

He sipped, grateful for the warm cup
in his hands. He looked over the papers

with the accusations,
but he did not sign them.

Think of your family, they said.
He thought of the lemon tree

outside the room where his sister slept
—its many little suns

lit by morning through the thick leaves.
He watched the darkness fall

and tried to remember the scent of lemons.
The night was long, staining the high window

he could not see out. *You are guilty*, they said,
You must sign. But he demurred.

One acceptance (the sweet coffee),
one refusal. Then nothing to think of

but the way the early light slanted
through the high window. Then

it was blue, though not as blue
as the guns, not as black as the scaffold.

Last Report

*

December. Shorter days again.
A long, low-pressure trough
hauling rain from Alaska and Hawaii.
Surprise of snow

on *oona-pa'is*, where long ago,
Coyote swept his feather
over the beginning of the world,
overturned his boat and spilled the springs
and creeks, the river and the wide floodplain,
and called the salmon home.

Knotted winds. Tangle of the lovers
hair, hands. Salty sweet their sleep.

Sunrise at 7:49. The waning Oak Moon
due west, a paring shy of round, bright
through the web of winter branches.

All day more clouds shoulder in.
Jet stream winds circle blue-green Earth
below the split polar vortex—
spinning Arctic cold south
over the lakes, spinning snow and ice
across the Great Plains.

In the Redwood Empire, local flooding
and road closures.
River cresting at midnight,
pouring into basements, climbing porches.

*

January. Moon of the Wolf,
moon of hunger. Sunrise at 7:19.
Waves higher than record
under furious winds. Ring of Fire
grumbling. Rodgers Creek Fault grinding
west of the Mayacamas.

Gray whales stitch air to ocean,
migrating north up the trench
outside Monterey Bay, their spouts
visible on the horizon.

Variable clouds thicken
into afternoon. Possible hail
as the fringe of a massive storm
heaves through, traveling
toward Colorado, South Dakota,
and the Twin Cities.

The long bones of darkness
settle early into evening
as geese settle over the marsh—
wings tucked, feathers fluffed
to insulate against the cold.

Low of 19 degrees.

The lovers turn in sleep—
face to face, breath to breath,
then back to back, legs touching,
feet touching.

High tide at 3 a.m.
Clouds passing quickly
across the hunger moon.

Warm under quilts, the lovers
curve together like sections of citrus—
hips, thighs, salty sweet.

*

January 29th. A cold wind
shoves the clouds up against
the Mayacamas. A flutter of snow
on the peaks, bright against gray grasses.

Deep in the rift zone,
under the surface of the Empire,
below the slip fault, tension builds—
in the hot zones of the body, tidal shifts
warming seas, hands, hips.

Uncertainty hinges between the breath,
in the space between factions,
between borders, migration, separation—
lost commons of belonging.

A black-tail doe trots along the side of the road,
looking for a break in the fence.

The current circles south.
Tsunami of plastic riding 5-foot swells
under the waning half moon.

The lovers rise early from the hum
of their dreams—to kettle whistle, morning
light. Branches lift to mostly sunny skies,
clouds passing quickly on the wind.
Highs in the 40s.

Sense of meaning trapped
in departmental syntax—more
euphemisms, greater abstraction,
longer lines. The genesis of violence.

    *

Kwong Roshi rakes the gravel path
to the zendo. Inside, he sits zazen
for all beings.

Increasing climate confusion.
Heavy equipment. Native seed suppression.
Lost commons of trust.

In the high country, the wolverine
shuffles hundreds of miles to the edge
of extinction.

    *

February 4th. Moon of the Long Snow.
Eagle feather adrift on a dry wind
over commute traffic.

Fast clouds at dusk. First stars.

The gray whales continue migrating north,
diving and rising, sea to air, air to sea.

Venus, Jupiter, Mars, and Saturn
align with the moon, marking a boundary.
Jupiter keeps his daughters close—
Io in her ice, Europa with her scarves
visible by Hubble. Distances
of space curving time to the moment.

From the mountains, Coyote chews his paw.

*

Mars sharpens his weapons
as the chaos deepens. Venus weeps
for lost sunsets and the suffering.

Assassination follows border conflict
on the sidewalk not far from his home
while walking the dog.

Cancellation of glacial melt monitoring.
Cancellation of news broadcast.
Monitoring of all persons
from birth by iris and microchip.

The dog howls for days
and tugs back to the spot.

The State claims no knowledge
of the incident.

Venus shivers without her golden shawl.
Heavy skies hang over the Empire.

Starbirth and the central nebula,
35,000 light-years across, the light
arriving now.

Coyote calls for a council.

*

The February Snow Moon gleams
over frosted rooftops. Overnight lows
of 18 to 20 degrees.

A split jet stream sends twin storms
spiraling over the Pacific,
their centers opaque and shapeless,
obscuring stars.

Sunrise at 7:08. Sunlight
creeps along the empty branches
and white bark of the birch tree,
climbing west toward the sea,
passing over the plastic gyre
wider than Texas.

Under the split polar vortex,
a jet stream 230 mph,
strongest ever recorded tailwind
cuts flight time from LA to Chicago.

The doe looks for a gap in the fence.

Privatization of air and water.
Mining and fracking of public land.
General brightness of observation,
halogens and artificial flowers.

The Snow Moon passes
over cliffs of granite and glaucophane,
passes over the dead whale on Bolinas Beach
whose eye had seen the stars

from mid-ocean, who had known
the gravitational paths of the planets
in the currents of the seas.

Blur of stars, their far light
still arriving after thousands of years.

Oh Great Swimmer, may you meet your kindred
on the other shore. May you swim forever
in safe seas.

　　*

March, and the Worm Moon of spring
passes through the Hunter's bright shoulders,
following Mars west an hour after sunset. Stars
humming all night over hips, thighs, the long
bones of darkness. Long

wave of the jet stream
weaving uncertainly south to Mexico,
then east, crossing the continent
and north up to Quebec—

followed by sunny skies.

Late March. The soil softens
under heavy rain throughout the day.
Local flooding. Earth a sponge,
too saturated, spills over.

Alder leaves like new-hatched butterflies
wave and flutter wet chartreuse wings.

Years ago, Coyote waved his feather
(once, twice, three times a charm)
over *oona-pa'is* and made the world,
tipped his boat and made
the seas and the creatures of the seas.

Coral reefs bleached white.
Pacific kelp gone.
Zooplankton homeless.

  *

May. The Flower Moon.

Coyote calls Bear and Fox. *Things are changing,*
he says. *Look down the mountain.* Together, they look
over the plain to the city, the freeway,
the lines of cars.

  *

Summer solstice. Sunrise at 5:48 a.m.
as the Moon of Strawberries sinks west.

Jupiter's moons, Saturn's rings, and Venus
with her golden sandals, her perfect pink toes,
sunrise walk across heaven—

Fukushima radiation found
in California wines.

Venus travels the night sky, sometimes near
but never touching Mars, or Jupiter,
never explaining. The silence of loss
steals her rosy apples and manges the hem
of her golden gown. She travels west
while Jupiter's daughters circle and spin.

*

Sunset at 8:17. A waning gibbous moon.
Lesser Lion roars with the winds
40 to 50 knots.

Blue light, blue heart.

Blurred stars guide the Ship of State.

*

Late summer. The moons of July and August—
days of harvest begin. First apples
the Gravensteins. The grandmothers bake
pies and make applesauce. The hills
darken from gold to gray. The Buck Moon
and the Sturgeon Moon pass.

Autumn, the Harvest Moon of September
passes into October and the Moon of the Hunter.

The time of fire deepens.

Surveillance of wildlands by firewatchers
day and night.

The Magellanic Clouds, once gauzy
and luminous, after midnight,
hidden by smoke.

Diablo Winds tunnel into firenados.
Showers of sparks fly down the hills
and over the houses of town.

At night, fire reddens the ridges
of the Mayacamas.
Deer run. Bear runs. Coyote
gnashes his teeth.

*

November. The Beaver Moon.
First rain. High tide near midnight.
The lovers

sigh and sleep, always touching—
lips, hands, rib to rib, back to back,
a tangle of trust as the Earth
turns toward morning, toward the whistle
of the kettle and the taste of tea.

Waves 8 to 10 feet. Wind 12 to 25 knots,
collars turned up. Autumn sun

spikes through clouds, across rooftops,
through the window, onto the red
Iranian rug. The days grow
shorter again.

Twilight, then night. Cradled
in the long bones of darkness,
under scattered showers,
the lovers sleep.
Above them, redwood branches
brush the roof, sweeping the darkness,
the wind an old woman
sweeping monastery steps.

Blue twilight. Smooth sheets,
bodies curved together—
unopened petals the color of moonlight.

They are two oars rowing the night sea
under the brush of branches,
sweeping the halls of sleep.

What have they forgotten,
sleeping so soundly under the rain,
rib to rib, under the sweep of branches,
wind caressing the eaves?

  *

December 1st. A single leaf clings
past its season, twists in the wind,
and flutters away. What remains
unsaid, the heart will speak. The ribs

of the stranded gray whale washed ashore
cradle a belly of eel grass and micro-beads,
tiny fragments of plastic toys and granules
of artificial turf.

The Moon of the Beaver travels west, sailing
over flocks of Sandpipers and Bar-tailed Godwits,
migrating the flyway over a rough Pacific.

Coyote could reconsider,
turn his boat back up, and travel north.
Or south toward the desert. He could
wave his feather again, couldn't he,
and take it all back?

The birch leaf flies upward. A river of wind
sweeps it high out over the town,
across the marsh, and west past the stars.

Rain gusts over the house
where the lovers sleep.
Breath and silence hold them.

Old and stiff with sadness, Saturn
sinks below the horizon.

    *

Winter again. A new year.
The Hunger Moon again.

All night the storm. High winds
meandering a massive low pressure trough
at the bottom of the stratosphere,
at the boundary with the troposphere.

Heedless and unwitting, once the boys
pulled the wings off a water-skate
to examine the fractal web,
then wondered at the stillness—
What have we done? Gone,

the tremor it made on quiet water—
first sense of sin. Sometimes he dreams
undoing the act, watches the water-skate
waft away over the pond.

How did life's meaning marry its grief?

When did love and death align?
How did such a design steal
into the pattern? What happened
that only the planets witnessed
from their divine distance?

The Hunger Moon howls outside
the lovers' window.

What is it that cannot be undone?

    *

February. Moon of the Long Snows.
2 a.m. Jupiter, Saturn, and Venus,
strung on a necklace, joined late
by the tired moon hidden in clouds.

Blue salt, blue lake of longing.

Mars in his dry red robes, with his voice of sand,
is silent. Nor do the stars speak.

Ah, moon—young and old, green
and ripe and rotting into darkness, into oblivion
and renewal. Ah, heart, hidden in so many guises.

Let me dream. Let the wind take me
with the last leaf dragged west
over the jagged edges of schist
or east on the current of the storm,
high in the clouds heavy with rain.
Let me leave behind
the world of salt and sorrow.

Let me unwind the wind, turn
toward the rebirth of stars, let the light
find its way back
to the heart of all origins.

*

March 26th. Sunrise at 6:41.
All day the clouds move east,
and green butterflies spin again
in the arms of alder.

Sky clear in the afternoon.

At 5:12, far below the whirling vortex winds,
the marsh ghosts rise from the wetlands
into the chill of dusk. Let me rise with them—

let me rise from the blue-black water,
let me rise from the bones of the whales,
let me rise from the skeletal shells
of once-a-multitude—clams, mussels,
and oysters dissolving in acidic seas,
foraminifera and copepods sinking
to the floor of the Pacific. Let me rise
with the marsh mist,
from the body of what I have loved.

Venus closes her lamp.
Ring of Fire roars under blue salt.

Merrily, Merrily

And sun trumpeting over the lines of traffic,
heavy and smothering in all that print,
no one pays any attention.

Dropping like flies now, the dogs the friends—
the water rising, the great dark coming.

The flowers bloom sweetly around the tipping stones.
No more shilly-shallying around the maypole.

We've seen the sagging flowers, stones aslant,
time nibbling away the names and dates.

Extinction

for Paul Shepherd

Even cold erodes, and the ice
that held itself in glacial cleaving
grows eager to lie down in the sea
where the great bears will finally sleep,
sliding quietly into the depths.
Their bones roll the bottom
in layers of darkness. What is left
besides light descending
into blue shadows, the billowing
curtains of salt, the slow heft of the sea?
How can we let what is lost
settle of its own weight
into the secret grief, the emptiness
we mistake for something missing
in ourselves?

In the Cities of Sleep

1.

When they spoke, we did not hear them.
Water, they said, and *salt,* their bright forms gritty with light.

   Water, salt, stone

The few that heard
and felt the sweep of light across their dreams
were silent, fearful of ridicule or exile.

Water, they sang with their great wet wings
of light or wind, and some heard
the sound of gunfire. Some heard rain.
Some heard the slow suspended drip
of a faucet or noticed nothing
beyond the fists we closed everywhere
over the earth.

   Water, salt, stone

2.

It was said the sea will rise,
the north soften and crumble,
and the great creatures of the old ice
will search in vain for their lodgings.

Then the winds will divide, driving sleet
over the plains and rain over the rivers,
and the land will slide away.

The wind will drive before it
the inheritors of our particulate air.

3.

The Dreamers will join the Rememberers,
and the Way will be sought from the patterns of the unseen.
This is why the record must be kept,
the auguries of bird and bone, of track and cloud.

4.

Salt—
          a whisper of wings,
a distant *sssssie* roar like the sea.

5.

So came we of the North with the wind
howling at our heels. The clean white gods
rarely spoke. Still we listened and puzzled
over the bones of reindeer, the tracks
of hare, the shapes of geese against the sky.

6.

In the South, it was already hot. Deserts blazed,
killing all but the lizards under the sand.

Late in the year, the sky held its breath.
Nothing stirred. The double-note cry of a hawk
slashed a warning.

The Earth shook herself,
breaching like an immense whale.
Then, swift as a murder of crows,
hot winds beat the branches low
toward the rumbling, rising Earth, our mother
who had been quiet so long,
we had all but forgotten her.

The women and children struggled
to reach each other, and the men too thrashed
toward their families. But the falling trees
and the groaning earth came between them.

7.

So came we of the West, the survivors of sickness,
with our prayers and our gods of fire, down
from the charred slopes into the lost centuries,
wandering season upon season, the moon
changing and changing, the winter branches
fracturing the horizon with black lightning.
Sunsets flooded the sky with the colors of fruit
and blood fading to iron.

8.

It may be when we are gone,
the white bears will once again swat seals
from the sea.

Only to those with the gift of remembering
or the gift of portent
will the revelation come.

Waking or sleeping, the Dreamers must tell us
the way of the Turning. The Seers must speak.

9.

I am told there are those who hear whispers
like the sound of the sea in the distance.
Sometimes they make out words,

    water
           salt
                    stone

words that sound like sighs
or like the beginning of rain
or a small cascade of scree. Some say

the whispers are a jumble of many voices,
many words. *Listen*, they command,
      river
            bird
                 rain—
though I myself have heard nothing
and cannot remember my dreams
and see only the fallen towers and flags
of the great cities of sleep.

Wind

A random tapping

around our midnight

conversation,

or was it prayer?

Memory, a backward story,

a slippery thing

like goodness

or evidence.

Once we were.

Was beautiful.

Hereafter

We chewed the bitter seeds
and separated and hoarded
and broke the pattern
and were punished with loss
and were lost to what we loved
and lay in the darkness, lonely
and un-entwined.

What We Stole

Barefoot rickshaw runners
breathing the street
carried us through air smelling of orchids,
cooking oil, exhaust from a thousand
two-cycle engines, the dark smoke
of plastic and trash—fires
the runners dodged as they hurled their bodies
ever forward, hauling us
over the roads of stone worn smooth by centuries.
We tied our scarves against the fatal air, bandits
come to raid what treasure they had—
carved statues of snakes and multi-armed gods,
the odd animals kept in cages,
the children whose labor we might claim
for our beds and our factories.
There was nothing we wanted
of their songs, their libraries
packed with notes from a long perished history
of thumbs and kings and common sorrows.
It was the strange we sought, the exotic secret
of their fabled happiness.

Fish Count in a Dry Year

Raccoon prints pock the ooze.
The mud smells of leaf-rot and dead fish.

Gray tufts stick up along the bank,
the grass mashed flat

under trees where deer have slept,
branches keeping the cold off their backs.

I follow the meander of last winter's water,
an empty bed of rocks and leaves

40 feet wide, the pools gone
except the one spring-fed—

the long lick of the dry creek
still flowing,

the way someone you love
remains after they die—the imprint
where you slept,

hours later,
when I turned on the light in the room.

November.
No rain.

I walk between what's missing
and what's here, counting

steelhead fry and the days since rain
and the lies I've told
and the times I cut my hair in grief.

Things settle—a leaf falls,

the white patches of light
from this November sky

tremble and still again

on the one abiding pool
under the alders.

Honey

What did you do when innocence died?
Denied it.

And then?
Mourned.

They nodded, turning
to each other. *Yes,*

haven't we all mourned?
Isn't that the crust of life? Yes,

and after that—
have you found the honey?

Oh, honey of life,
barely begun—

I turned and found the empty
apse filled with bees,

a hive of golden wax,
a smear of pollen on my hands.

All Day It Was
about Distances

First the flash of a hawk, the space
between air and earth
narrowing, something breathless

in its twist as it dove,
south autumn sun
through rust-hued feathers,

to disappear
in the dark, collapsed grass—
late in the day, a maple leaf

edged against 4 o'clock sky
scuttered across the road,
end-over-end,

close to the ground, fast,
just a glimpse.
Now in the night garden,

amid roses guarded by armies of thorns,
the dog prowling dark
for the hide-and-seek cat,

the moon behind clouds,
a milky patch in galactic black.
I stand listening.

You in your bed, guarded
by your own armies, dreaming
or near the surface of sleep,

with all the distance of your fears
inside you and the long roads of loss
crossed and re-crossed

by slow caravans of hope. I listen
to the worn harness and buckles and bells
fade in the distances we live with—

the hunger of the poor,
the ravaged cities. I listen
for the steady cricket song
of the heart's secret,
the broken stumbling scuff
of our reaching wings.

Holy Day of winter

Blessed be the frost that lingers into afternoon.
Blessed be the blind roots weaving.
Blessed be the patient bulbs.
Blessed be the promise of seeds splitting and sprouting.
Blessed be the nubs of leaves and hope opening.
As sunlight dissolves distance, let us touch.
As pilgrims bent to holy ground, touch.
As earth welcomes rain, touch.
Blessed be our body.
Blessed be the silence that opens the heart.

Safe Harbor

The older cat
still manages to jump onto the bed,
though he topples on the rough sea
of the humped quilt and stranded pillows
where you propped your left knee
over your right, another
for your shoulder. The cat

settles between us, tucking his nose
into the black tip of his tail.

Last night's rain
still falls

one drop at a time
from the overhanging branches.

Here's the thing, the cat says,
my branch of the evolutionary tree—

he lifts his head
to let you scratch his chin. Our little sea
with its safe harbor. The waters of the world

are all connected, as the forests
with their now-famous mycorrhizal web.
The Japanese fisherman

hauls in his catch,
as a child slips overboard
in the Mediterranean.

A gray whale glides south
through a school of micro-plastic,
mouth open, trusting.

A sixty-year-old albatross flies ten-thousand miles
to dance and lay her egg
on Midway Island; her chick

feeds on cigarette filters
found in the dunes.

.

From the rigging
of an oil platform, a man
climbs down, turning his chapped face
from the North Sea wind.

Across the small chaos
of our bed, the cat stretches
one paw toward you, closes his eyes,
and sleeps.

Meanwhile, Music

Tree to tree, the birds fly to perch and sing
amid the sway and swing of spring's busy wind,
while wars go on, while the sea rises and the ice melts.

In the midst of life, narrowing to the onyx box,
the house of Anubis side by side with the house of music,
sun blesses the breakfast table.

All is perishing, and yet they sing—they sing.

Bringing Back Water

That night, you went down the street
to bring back water—sweet
smell of rain
on your shirt, the good water
from who-knows-where
in its killer-plastic bottle. Wind
through the open door, leaving,
returning. Now stars
too early for the old moon.
There is a wilderness of pure joy
beneath all sorrow.
It's where things begin.

NOTES

The Goldilocks Zone refers to Earth's distance from the sun, a distance that allows for a habitable global temperature. The Goldilocks Zone is the range of distance with the right temperatures for water to remain liquid.

Solastalgia combines two words: *solacium* (comfort) and *algia* (pain, suffering or grief). Originally coined by Australian environmental researcher Genn A. Albrecht, it refers to the suffering of no longer feeling at home where one lives. It is currently being used to describe a syndrome of human distress related to environmental change (generally degradation) and a sense of homesickness while still being present in or connected to one's home environment. https://pubmed.ncbi.nlm.nih.gov/18027145/

Swan Bone—Paleolithic flutes have been found dating back over 40,000 years. These ancient flutes have been carved from a variety of bones, including bear bones, vulture bones, mammoth bones, and the wing-bone of a swan.

Report was written over a period of many months, reading the daily report of weather, tides, planetary movements, the moon cycle, records of temperature and rainfall. At some point, I realized I was looking at a complicated series of interdependent, interrelated cycles that might be thought of as musical. It struck me that, all over the world, there are cultures whose art is a reflection of the complexity of Earth's natural systems—gamelan music in Asia, African drumming, Celtic knot work and designs, Polish basket weaving. I began to appreciate these as expressions of ecological wisdom, metaphors of the relationships between all these cycles, diurnal and seasonal patterns within patterns. I wanted to convey the sensuality I felt inherent in the complicated interplay of these systems. Crucially, I wanted to present the insignificance of human life within nature's magnitude, a point of view I found in Inuit poetry. *Oona-pa'is* is the name given to Sonoma Mountain by the Indigenous people of Sonoma County; Coyote made the world from the top of *oona-pa'is,* Sonoma Mountain.

BETWEEN—United States Institute of Peace, July 2021, report has found that "our planet's warming is weakening already fragile states, increasing the risk of violent conflicts and accelerating human displacement and migration." Floods and drought, sea level rise and hotter temperatures—all predictable effects of the warming climate—are destabilizing the Middle East, Southeast Asia, Central Africa, and the Dry Corridor of Central America. A key underlying condition of conflict in Iraq, Afghanistan, and Syria is drought. These countries were largely agricultural until years-long drought brought food scarcity and forced people to abandon their farms and migrate to the cities. Stress conditions have activated latent inter-group hostilities as well as civil unrest and increasingly repressive government policies. The Climate Change and Migration Coalition reports that a hotter planet means more armed conflict. Similarly, according to the Council on Foreign Relations Global Conflict Tracker, as of June 2021, reports of armed conflicts are ongoing and expanding. Fighting continues on the Nigerian border and in the Cameroonian civil war; insurgent attacks persist in Mozambique; Boko Haram wreaks havoc in Nigeria's northeast. Millions of people are caught in violence in the Tigray region of Ethiopia.

Farther south, in the Sahel of Central Africa, conflicts are more acute than ever between the agrarian and pastoral peoples that have historically shared the land seasonally by turns. As a result of prolonged drought, starvation in the Sahel has reached such proportions that, in 2023, we have daily reports of the deaths, especially of children, as people leave their territories and wander from village to village in search of water and food. According to ProPublica, "The Great Climate Migration" has already begun.

February Freeze—An Eritrean man had been trying to join a friend in Switzerland for seven years but could not get papers that would allow him to leave Eritrea. In desperation, he stowed away in the wheel well of a Boeing 747 destined for England and froze to death. His body fell when the landing gear was lowered ahead of arrival.

Dial Face is dedicated to Ken Saro-Wiwa, the Ogoni activist who led demonstrations against Dutch Shell Oil in Ogoni tribal land, where thousands of breaks in the poorly maintained oil pipelines have led to the despoiling of massive areas of Ogoniland in the Niger Delta. Frequent explosions along the pipeline are responsible for the deaths of hundreds of people, and spills choke the wetlands, killing fish, destroying the livelihood of delta fishing people. Saro-Wiwa was a writer and media producer. He was executed by the Nigerian government in collusion with Dutch Shell Oil in 1995. The face of a gasoline pump is known as the "dial face."

Eremocene or Age of Loneliness is the term coined by American biologist E. O. Wilson (1929-2021), who is known for popularizing sociobiology. One of his primary concerns was massive human induced species losses.

Ghost Dance—in the late nineteenth century, Native American peoples across much of the western United States incorporated into their traditional dances the Ghost Dance intended to bring contact with the spirit world, especially to call on the spirits of the ancestors to bring Native American peoples throughout the region together and aid them in the effort to overcome European-American oppression and westward expansion.

The Virus on Good Friday—When Covid swept across the country, gradually it became known that many more people of color were dying than white people. In Chicago, the breakdown was eight out of ten. Structural racism in healthcare had never before been so blatantly apparent. Throughout the first year of Covid, there were videos posted by people all over the world to show how they were coping with quarantine and isolation. Several videos from Russia showed how ballerinas there were practicing at home. In one such video, the dancers were holding pots and pans in place of partners.

While Bombs Fell—Russian General Sergey Surovikin, who ordered both the bombing of Aleppo, Syria, and the bombing of Grozny, Chechnya, is currently (as of December 2022) in charge of the Russian assault on Ukraine.

Strike, to do the digging—The constant bombing of Aleppo by the Russian military in support of Syrian government forces left too many bodies to bury. "Even if I were to consider mass burials, I don't have the machines to do the digging," local forensic authority, Aleppo, Syria,

December 2016.

Nesting—Italicized sections are from *The Poetics of Space* by Gaston Bachelard. The child's death referenced near the end of the poem was an incident reported in the news. Other scraps of news reports are scattered throughout the poem. The red-dyed egg of the last lines is from a Greek Easter custom; thus the hands are held as if in prayer. Like many religious practices, however, its origin is older than Christianity; the red egg likely long represented the blood of birth and sacrifice for new life in traditional rituals associated with spring.

A Woman Lies Still—is dedicated to Nobel Prize-winning human rights lawyer Oleksandra Matviichuk, who has said the Russian invasion of Ukraine is a genocide. In her role as a witness to human rights violations, Matviichuk says the Russian atrocities in Ukraine are greater than any she has seen anywhere, and she says, "Never have I seen greater pain."

Children of War: Daughter was inspired by a photograph that appeared in the New York Times of a mother in Iraq, standing at the foot of her daughter's hospital bed. Her daughter had been severely burned in the thermal wave of a bomb blast. Likewise, *Brother* arose from something I read about the radicalization of children whose family members have been killed or injured in armed conflict.

Cell Songs—Protein music (DNA music or genetic music) is a conversion of the protein sequence of a cell into musical notes. Incidents cited in the poem are taken from various news reports from the Middle East.

If Only—In various Coyote stories among Indigenous people

of western North America, Coyote brings gifts but also trouble. In one famous story, he steals fire from the sun. Because he is greedy and always hungry, Coyote is also known to nibble his own tail or eat a paw.

Smoke—With drought and increasingly higher air and soil temperatures in the western United States, wildfires have become more frequent and more intense, burning thousands of miles of wildland and encroaching on human settlements. Simultaneously, migration from the southern hemisphere is on the rise. During the administration of President Donald Trump, the policy of "zero tolerance" and family separation along the southern border began as a pilot project in 2017. By 2018, it had led to the incarceration of thousands of children, separated from their parents and held in wire cages for weeks and sometimes months at a time. Long before the Trump administration implemented its zero tolerance immigration enforcement policy in 2018, it was already separating children from their parents in the El Paso, Texas, area and along other sections of the border. Children held under the family separation policy suffer profound and lasting psychological damage from the experience.

Winter Pilgrims—In the winter of 2021, several thousand migrants were transported to Belarus and left in the woods near the Polish border. It was bitterly cold, and these people had only what they had been able to carry. Unprepared for their arrival, Poland put up rolls of barbed-wire fencing and ordered troops to guard the border. Belarus refused to allow aid agencies into the country, and Poland was adamant that the migrants not be allowed in. Because of exposure and lack of supplies, there were deaths among the migrants. The situation was on the news, and all over the world, images of the migrants flashed from phones, televisions, and computer screens for several weeks. It is still not known how many people may have died there.

Here Now—Babi Yar is the Russian name of a ravine where one of the world's greatest single-incident atrocities occurred in 1941, when German Nazis executed nearly 34,000 Ukranian Jews in an effort to kill all the Jews in Kyiv. The site continued to be used as a place for executions, and today, it has been estimated that some 100,000 people died there. Before World War II, during the Holomodor, Josef Stalin starved nearly four million Ukrainians after seizing the wheat grown on Ukrainian farms and shipping it to Russia.

The High Window—Majid-Reza Rahnavard, a 23-year-old protestor, was arrested after participating in demonstrations against the Iranian government. He was held for just ten days, summarily tried (accused of killing two secret agents), found guilty by the Iranian Revolutionary Court, and publicly hung from a construction crane on December 8, 2022, in the city of Mashhad.

Last Report—Returning to oceanographic, meteorological, and weather records a decade after *Report*, the whisper of global warming had become a roar, and the actual impact of humanity on the Earth, primarily through the climate crisis, is reflected throughout the weave of nature. These marked changes in the patterns meant an accurate *Report* would have to include more of humanity. Thus, *Last Report* is peppered with references to "the lovers" who appeared only three times in the first *Report*. Sparse references to news of the day are included. To my complete surprise, I found myself drawn directly into the poem toward the end. Among the most ominous changes are the erratic behavior of the jet stream winds and the storms they bring. For the first time in all my observation, I saw the jet stream split into twin storms over the Eastern Pacific, with two storm eyes, their centers blurred and disorganized. Other anomalies of the jet stream have moved bodies of hot and of cold air in unusual patterns affecting rainfall, storms, and off-shore wind speeds. The splitting of the Polar Vortex, those winds above the jet stream that circle the North Pole, keeping a lid on the Arctic cold, is another development. As the Arctic continues to warm (more rapidly than anywhere on Earth), the Polar Vortex has split, allowing winter storms to sweep freezing temperatures across wide swaths of the continent in bomb cyclones. The greater frequency and intensity of these massive storms is attributed to climate change, as are more frequent intense hurricanes. Diablo winds and "firenados" are local phenomena also attributed to global warming, which has dried both soil and plants, as well as the air, leaving California and other parts of the West especially vulnerable to wildfire. The troposphere is the atmospheric area below the stratosphere where most of the activity of wind and moisture occurs. Global warming has brought unrest across the planet in areas where drought, flooding, heat waves, and major storm events are making it clear that human activity has a far greater impact on nature than ever before. We may have passed the tipping point in the feedback of melting permafrost and the lethal release of methane. For the first time in human history, we have to acknowledge human activity may destroy the very natural systems life depends upon. To account for these shifts in the human impact on nature, *Last Report* includes numerous references to the human realm. This shift also reflects changes in my own life, as the population of Sonoma County has doubled along with increases in development. Extensive new rural fencing prevents hiking through the old orchards and turns backroads into corridors of death for wildlife. Development and fencing limit people from the experience of themselves as part of the surrounding natural world, just as the natural world is further separated from humans. Interactions between the two become cause for surprise or alarm rather than supporting a feeling of connection and kinship.

The title, *Merrily, Merrily*, refers to the jaunty nineteenth-century nursery rhyme: *Row row row your boat, gently down the stream. Merrily, merrily, merrily, merrily, life is but a dream.*

Extinction—Paul Howe Shepherd, Jr, PhD (1925-1996) called himself a human ecologist and wrote numerous books about the human relationship to nature. His ideas were a melding of anthropology, philosophy, and ecology. Sometimes called an environmentalist, his contributions to the field of deep ecology argued that humans are developmentally dependent upon nature and that, in the absence of wild animals and wild places, humans are lonely and lack a sense of belonging (*The Others, How Animals Made Us Human*).

ACKNOWLEDGMENTS

I am especially indebted to the editors who selected earlier versions of some of the poems in this book and who encouraged me to keep working, even while the subject of global warming brought difficult feelings of grief and despair. My writing has been an antidote to that despair, and the friends, editors, and publishers who were not afraid of my grief have been essential to the writing and completion of this book.

Barrett Warner, editor at *Free State,* welcomed my wildest work and took the time to write back when he rejected some and took some. Ray Waddle, editor of *Reflections,* responded to my earlier poems so kindly that I took heart and continued my work; thanks to him, I was able to write about the fires that threaten our homes here in Sonoma County. Thanks to *KickAss Review; Psychological Perspectives, a Quarterly Journal of Jungian Thought; Comstock Review; West Marin Review; Whistling Shade; On the Commons; Center for Humans and Nature; Ecological Citizen; Jung Journal of Culture and Psyche,* and *Free State Review* for supporting me by publishing my work.

Among the friends whose support has been critical to the making of this book, first and foremost is my husband, Brendan Smith, who listens, acknowledges, and supports my every effort, who knows just how long to wait before critical comment so my thinking is not cut short by doubt, and who tolerates my distraction when I'm preoccupied for long hours that can turn into days. I also want to thank Ann Hancock, who showed me we can think about climate from a can-do perspective, who amazes me in more ways than I can count, and who, without intending to, shows me what the best looks like. Thanks to Suze Cohan for making space for my books to meet their readers. Thanks to Susan Tillett for faith in me and for offering the perfect small suggestions. Thanks to Kim and Clay Clement for being there in the best and the worst of times with love and good advice. Thanks to Jack Crimmins for inspiration to trust the first thoughts. Thanks to Ute Scott-Smith for good company before and during the pandemic. Thanks to Julia and Anna and Cary for showing me what a good neighbor is. Thanks to dearest Chach for her deep intelligence, her humor, and her ever-loving presence. Thanks to my cousin, Patricia Bowen, for her willingness to share the search, to Susan and Rick Matteson for years of generosity in every way, to Joan Ayers for resilience and for a model of love with no strings attached. Thanks to the Writers Group and the Choir. Thanks to the Poet Laureate Committee for selecting me to serve; thanks to Clara Rosemarda for nominating me. Steady thanks as always to Mike Traynor, old friend, someone to live up to. And to my beloved animal companions, living and no longer whinnying with us: Nick, Jagger, Buddy, Trellie, Samba, and Cesar.

The following poems received publication as indicated:

"In the Cities of Sleep" appeared in *Kickass Review* and later in *Jung Journal.*

"Man Found on Fire" was published by *Free State Review*

"Extinction," *Canary, a Literary Journal of the Environmental Crisis.*

"Bringing Back Water," *Uncommon Word* and later in *Sisyphus.*

"February Freeze," *Free State Review.*

"Report," from *dPress.*

"All Day It Was About Distances," *Whistling Shade.*

"On Fire," *Reflections.*

TITLE INDEX

First Line Index

A

B

D

E

F

H

www.ingramcontent.com/pod-product-compliance
Lightning Source LLC
Chambersburg PA
CBHW010857090426
42737CB00020B/3401